RAPHAEL

By MARIA GRAZIA CIARDI DUPRÉ

AVENEL BOOKS

NEW YORK

Raffaello © MCMLXXIX by Fabbri Editori, Milan, Italy
English Translation Copyright © by Fabbri Editori, Milan, Italy
All Rights Reserved
First U.S. Edition published 1979 by Avenel Books
distributed by Crown Publishers Inc.
Printed in Italy by Fabbri Editori, Milan.
b   c   d   e   f   g   h   i

Traslation by STEPHEN SARTARELLI

Library of Congress Cataloging in Publication Data
Raphael, 1483-1520.
Raphael.
Translation of Raffaello.
1. Raphael, 1483-1520—Catalogs. I. Ciardi Duprè
dal Poggetto, Maria Grazia.
ND623.R2A4 1979 759.5 78-71506
ISBN 0-517-277913

Raffaello Sanzio was born in 1483 into an age named for its creative spirit and accomplishments. Only thirty-seven years later, he died, having become in his brief lifespan one of the sublime creators of that age. Raffaello's father, Giovanni Santi, was himself a painter, though of modest gifts. He was quick to recognize his son's abilities and began training him early in the classical principles of painting and architecture.

Raffaello learned, too, from the celebrated master Pietro Perugino, whose studio in Perugia he visited in company with his father. Another preceptor – though simply through the influence of his works – was Piero della Francesca, whose paintings hung in the palace in Urbino, the city where Raffaello spent his childhood.

With the death of Giovanni Santi in 1494, Raffaello found himself orphaned, and shortly thereafter he left Urbino to accept work as an apprentice in the workshop of Pietro Perugino. At fourteen he collaborated with Perugino on a major work, the predella of the S. Maria Nuova altarpiece.

Understandably, Raffaello's first important works show the influence of this mentor. All were executed for the noble courts of Perugia and Città di Castello. The first to be documented was an altarpiece, now lost except for a few fragments, commemorating the coronation of St. Nicholas of Tolentino. Raffaello was seventeen when he accepted the commission for the altarpiece, to be done in collaboration with another painter. A sheet of admirable drawings for the work, made by Raffaello, remains in existence. The "S. Nicola Altarpiece" represented a coming of age for Raffaello.

Henceforth he accepted commissions for himself alone, most of them in the cities of Perugia and Città di Castello. His ambition and energy were boundless. At the end of 1501 he finished the "S. Nicola Altarpiece" and the following year began the "Coronation of the Virgin" for the Church of S. Francesco in Perugia. In 1503 he depicted in the Church of S. Francesco in Città di Castello a Crucifixion, now called the "Mond Crucifixion", and for the same church in the following year he created the magnificent "Marriage of the Virgin".

Having thus helped to raise the curtain on the glorious sixteenth century, the Cinquecento of Italian art, in 1504 the young man moved to Florence, where he applied himself passionately to the study of Florentine art and to the further development of this own style. These years saw the execution of some of his greatest masterpieces – in the "Conestabile Madonna", the "Lady of the Unicorn", the "Granduca Madonna", the "Small Cowper Madonna", the Belvedere Madonna", the "Orléans Madonna", the "Madonna of the Goldfinch", "La Belle Jardinière", the Doni portraits, and the Canigiani "Holy Family", among others. This activity did not hinder him from executing several major works in Perugia in the same period. They included the "Ansidei altarpiece", the "Colonna altarpiece", the "Deposition", and the fresco "Christ in Glory and the Saints".

In Rome, meanwhile, Julius II had begun his energetic reign as Pope, intent on consolidating the power of the Church. He envisaged a Vatican breathtaking in its grandeur, and he commis-sioned the finest artists of the day to make it so. Thus it was inevitable that Raffaello would go to Rome, which he did toward the end of 1508.

With the approval of Bramante, architect of the papal palaces, Raffaello began a prodigious series of frescoes in the papal apartments, the rooms known as the Stanze Vaticane. As work progressed on the first room, the Stanza della Segnatura, it became evident to the men of letters and Humanists of the court that they were in the presence of genius. Given the theme of the four faculties – Theology, Law, Philosophy, and the Poetic Arts – Raffaello translated them into an art that was new although with a strong classical foundation – an art both powerful and refined. With the completion of the Stanza della Segnatura, Raffaello moved with equal vigor to the second of the papal rooms, the Stanza d'Eliodoro. The frescoes there, each one an historical narrative, are charged with drama, with the interplay of light and shadow, and with unusual color treatments.

Raffaello's work at this time was not confined to the Vatican walls. His embellishments of churches and villas included the "Madonna of Foligno", the "Galatea" fresco in the Villa Farnesina, and the famous "Madonna of the Chair".

By 1514 the Stanza d'Eliodoro was completed, Leo X had succeeded Julius as Pope, and Raphael had entered a new, indeed, the final phase of his life, during which he depended more ad more on assistants for the execution of his designs. He extended his labors to include the responsibility of serving as official architect for the new construction work on St. Peter's. It was the highest appointment to which an artist in Rome could aspire. Raffaello was now without peer in the city; Bramante was dead, and Michelangelo, who had completed his work on the ceiling of the Sistine Chapel, had left Rome to return to Florence.

Raffaello applied himself to many diverse projects during the last six years of his life. To his collaborators he entrusted the execution of his designs for the Third Stanza Vaticana, the Stanza dell'Incendio, frescoes with motifs reflecting the Humanist preoccupations of the papal court. As an architect, he was perhaps able to exercise his taste and skill more readily for private patrons than for the Vatican, where funds and enthusiasm for building had waned after the passing of Julius. Raffaello's many other activities included the depicting and mapping of ancient Rome, cartoons for tapestries to be woven in Brussels and hung on the walls of the Sistine Chapel, and a number of portraits, frescoes, and religious works. The paintings include the last great works to be executed in his own hand, among them "St. Cecilia", the "Christ Falling on the Way to Calvary", the Louvre's "St. Michael", and the "Transfiguration".

Raffaello died on April 6, 1520, of an acute fever, but perhaps more truly of exhaustion from a too intense and ardent life. The feelings of his contemporaries, including his students, may be guessed from this comment in a letter: "The air of heaviness in the porticoes (of the Vatican) this week was not because the palace of the pontificate has of late been so threatened... it was an omen that he who so embellished it was about to be missed".

Raffaello was buried in the Pantheon in Rome.

The glorious adventure of the ''modern manner'' from Urbino to Rome

Portrait of a young man (thought to be a self-portrait) - Oxford, Ashmolean Museum

With the reordering of Raffaello's early works as a result of postwar scholarship, the artist has taken on a more real, more human aspect. An important group of paintings, once thought to be the prodigies of a flawless youth, has been shown to be from the period about 1505, when Raffaello was already considered a ''master''. Raffaello's first years of artistic production are thus revealed as a time of prudent development under the instruction of teachers such as Pietro Perugino and possibly Pinturicchio, and influenced strongly by the heritage of Piero della Francesca.

These experiences are evident in the first known works of the artist: a double-faced standard in Città di Castello depicting the ''Madonna della Misericordia'' and the ''Crucifixion''; a fresco ''Madonna with Child'', in his father's house in Urbino, and the altarpiece of ''S. Nicola di Tolentino'', lost today except for some fragments. Stylistically akin to the S. Nicola altarpiece is the small but marvelous ''Resurrection'' now in Sâo Paulo. From this work the progression moves easily to works of astonishing mastery: the ''Coronation of the Virgin'', the ''Mond Crucifixion'', the ''Marriage of the Virgin'', and numerous other paintings all done by 1504. The double-faced standard in Città di Castello is the most obvious indication of Raffaello's interest in the art of Piero della Francesca. His exposure to this master established in his art certain fundamental elements: the limpid measurement of space, the intense luminosity of chiaroscuro, and the ability to alternate solids and voids, as on a fabric.

All the other works of this period reveal the influence of Perugino. We see it particularly in the ''Coronation of the Virgin'', in the composition, the movement of the figures, the faces, and the drapery. And yet, as jakob Burckhardt has observed, Raffaello was able to give the painting ''the sweetness of devotion, the beauty of youth, the enthusiasm of the aged, and all with a purely celestial manner which the master (Perugino) never achieved. Moreover, the design and drapery are incomparably more exact.'' Vasari, writing of the ''Mond Crucifixion'', says: ««If he hadn't signed it, nobody would believe it to be the work of Raffaello, but rather of Perugino.'' But the soft and graceful modeling in this work seems classically

5

Greek, demonstrating that the artist was already inclined toward that purity which he was to perfect in his later Florentine works.

In his sublime "Marriage of the Virgin", Raffaello has developed these qualities so far as to surpass Perugino. The lucid spatial arrangement that distinguishes this painting became the hallmark of the young Raffaello. The coloring, with its clear and resplendent luminosity, confers on the human form a purity worthy of ancient Greek classicism. In contrast, Perugino wraps his figures in chiaroscuro, as though veiled with smoke from some unseen source. Nevertheless, Raffaello's debt to the master was considerable, since he learned from him the delicately undulating compositional rhythm that had been one of the important characteristics of Perugino's Neoclassicism.

According to his early biographer, Vasari, Raffaello's glorious adventure really began when, "spurred by the love that he always had for excellence in art", he arrived in Florence late in the year 1504. Here his eyes were opened; the young painter, "who thought he had already accomplished much, found this to be far from true." The reputation of "master", which he had won in the provinces, faded in the face of the great artistic events of Renaissance Florence. At the time he arrived, Michelangelo and Leonardo had already completed a group of works that were to become the foundations of the new art of the Cinquecento. Leonardo had already painted the Louvre "St. Anne", Michelangelo had sculpted the "Bruges Madonna", the "David", and the "Tondo Pitti", among others, and had painted the "Tondo Doni". The two artists were at work secretly on the two famous cartoons, now unfortunately lost, of the "Battle of Cascina" and the "Battle of Anghiari". Another power in the artistic life of Florence was the painter Fra' Bartolommeo, who had quickly assimilated the new styles of Leonardo and Michelangelo and had demonstrated them by adding fullness of modeling, unity of color, and breadth of composition to the soft classicism of the Quattrocento, so well exemplified by Perugino.

Raffaello found himself no longer a master, but once again a disciple. "Anyone else might have lost heart", wrote Vasari. "Even someone equally talented would have never done what Raffaello did... With incredible application for one of such tender years... he did his utmost to accomplish in a few months that which would have needed years to do had he already been a man." Fra' Bartolommeo, Leonardo, and Michelangelo, respectively, represent the stages that Raffaello traversed as he made his way into the vanguard of the Cinquecento painters. The works he executed in Florence and Perugia in the four years from the end of 1504 to the end of 1508 bear witness to the exceptional success of his efforts.

He turned first to Fra' Bartolommeo, probably because of certain affinities of temperament and culture; both had had their starting point in Pietro Perugino, though each interpreted that master's influence differently. In Raffaello's first work of this period, the "Conestabile Madonna", Fra' Bartolommeo's manner is recalled by the simplicity of the group, but its placement against the landscape is carried out with a new breadth of feeling; the chiaroscuro of the Perugino form here loses its inertia and begins to open up, to become animated.

The solid and resplendent presence of the subject in the "Lady of the Unicorn" harks back to the celebrated "Last Judgment" of Fra' Bartolommeo. Raffaello studied this fresco at great length during his stay in Florence, and it influenced his style in both the "Colonna Altarpiece" and the fresco of the "Trinity and the Saints". Bartolommeo's Flemish preciosity is visible in Raffaello's many small paintings of this period, such as "The Vision of a Knight", the "St. George" in the National Gallery in Washington, the diptych of "St. Michael and St. George", and "The Three Graces". At one time all these were believed to be among Raffaello's earliest works. From the proper viewpoint, however, one can see in these pointings that Bartolommeo liberated Raffaello from Perugino's seductive conventionality. The modeling has gained breadth and fluidity, movement is articulated decisively, and gestures and expressions are increasingly true to life. The landscape, which in Perugino had static serenity, is enlivened with clues to the hour of day and the variation of seasons. As Vasari so acutely describes the "Conestabile Madonna": "The wind still blows cold from the azure sky and from the hills white with snow; the wan green countryside has been barely touched by the first breath of spring." In the "St. George" in the Louvre, spring has just arrived, clothing some of the trees with tender leaves and the earth with a cloak of unripe green; the sky is blanched by a veil of

Group of drawings of the Madonna and Child - London, British Museum

fog. In the ''St. George'' in the National Gallery in Washington the dense trees tell us that summer has come.

The new stylistic aspects and expressiveness that came to light in these first Florentine works were not, however, departures from the ideal of beauty that had governed Raffaello's Perugino period. This ideal, to which the painter remained faithful all his life, was based on the classical laws of harmony, symmetry and proportion. The scholar Venturi has pointed out how, in ''The Thee Graces'', ''the elliptical contour, which encloses the three figures in a light embrace, repeats itself like an echo in the serpentine twistings of the river, in the curves of the plain, all the way to the horizon bathed in the dawn's white light.'' And numerous such examples could be given.

This ideal of beauty supported Raffaello during the profound changes he underwent as a result of his encounters with Leonardo and Michelangelo. Nearly all the paintings of his Florentine period demonstrate a preoccupation with composition and form, though he never failed to give each work his characteristic delicate emotional tone.

The influence of Leonardo begins to show in the portraits, ''Guidobaldo da Montefeltro'' and his wife ''Elisabetta Gonzaga''. Stylistically they have elements in common with the ''Colonna Altarpiece'', but behind ''Elisabetta Gonzaga'' we discern Raffaello's first Leonardo background. After this came the ''Terranuova Madonna'', which reveals elements taken from Leonardo's early and mature periods: in the form of the Madonna's face and in the more intense contrast created by the light *chiaro* on the clotted mass of colors, which now functions as darkness *scuro*. But whenever Raffaello concedes to an outside influence, he transforms the new idea and makes it his own. This is true not merely of the ''Terranuova Madonna'', but of his entire artistic activity. Venturi's analysis is helpful: where ''the kneeling 'Virgin of the Rocks' of Leonardo leans to one side, thus weakening the architectural stability of the whole, Raffaello's Virgin towers in the sky and Coordinates all the elements of the painting with... her gestures... Leonardo's Madonna has shadows for background, and it seems almost as if she wants to lose herself in them; Raffaello's shines immobile in the luminous sphere of the heavens.''

In the celebrated ''Granduca Madonna'', where the Virgin slowly moves out of a black background, faintly smiling, the influence of Leonardo is even more obvious. The compositional design and soft drapery of this work place it at the head of a brilliant group of paintings closely linked by similarities of style. The most important, in probable chronological order, are the "Holy Family" and the "Orléans Madonna", both of which contain the same archaic type of draper, and the "Small Cowper Madonna": in the latter the brushstrokes fluidly trace the undulating folds of the draperies, attesting to Raffaello's study of a more advanced stage of Leonardo's painting, the period represented by the "St. Anne" of the Louvre.

If Raffaello was in fact able to study the "St. Anne", he probably also knew the cartoon for this painting, which is now in the National Gallery in London. The influence of this masterpiece can also be seen in the "Madonna of the Goldfinch" and in "La Belle Jardinière" of 1507. In "La Belle Jardinière", in keeping with the stylistic innovations of Leonardo's cartoon, the movement loses its undulating and interlaced pattern to find expression in the greatest possible breadth of form. The perfect harmony between measurements, surfaces and color brings the amplified Leonardo forms to a perfection at once poised, heavenly and still very natural.

These stylistic achievements prepared Raffaello for his encounter with Michelangelo. The first contact took place when Raffaello was commissioned to paint the portrait of Agnolo Doni. In this man's home Raffaello was finally able to see and become familiar with the "Holy Family" tondo, the only example of Michelangelo's painting then in existence. That a revelation took place is proved by the profound stylistic change which occurred in Raffaello's art between "La Belle Jardinière" and "The Deposition", both of 1507.

In "The Deposition" the Holy Woman kneeling at the right, twisting as she attempts to support the Blessed Virgin, is a precise reference – the first – to the "Tondo Doni" of Michelangelo. Other motifs in this work, such as the body of Jesus, derive from Michelangelo's sculpture. But Michelangelo's greatest influence was in revealing to Raffaello the vast possibilities of historical scenes. This altarpiece of Raffaello's is not simply a depiction of a group of figures. For the first time, his subject is the action itself, an historical event; not a *pietà*, but the actual carrying of the dead Christ to the tomb. "The Deposition" raised the curtain on the historical mode of painting that would be Raffaello's great achievement during his years in Rome.

Raffaello's desire to paint historical subjects was a reaction to Michelangelo's treatment of dynamics. This is proved by the large group of drawings that evidence the laborious genesis of "The Deposition". These drawings pass from the static formula of "Mourning", based on the model of Fra' Bartolommeo, to studies of dramatic and historical action. This development came as Raffaello contemplated Michelangelo's treatment of action – though it must be said that for Michelangelo, action was portrayed as ideal, timeless and hence outside of history. Raffaello once again proved himself able to answer mastery with mastery, transforming and enlarging upon that which previously had seemed perfect and complete.

Once in Rome, Raffaello's long accumulation of knowledge and experience combined with the new vistas opening up to him and history became the great theme of this work. He achieved his masterwork in this genre with the decoration of the Stanze Vaticane. He worked with passionate dedication on the first two, the "Stanza della Segnatura" and the "Stanza d'Eliodoro", from 1509 to 1514. Then his many commitments forced him to entrust to his students the execution of the third, the "Stanza dell'Incendio". They completed it in 1517. The fourth, the "Stanza di Costantino", was carried out after his death.

Noble concepts were chosen as the subjects for the Stanza decorations. The frescoes in the "Stanza della Segnatura" illustrated the pursuits through which man may attain perfection: Justice, Poetry, Philosophy and Theology. Justice was represented by the figures of Fortitude, Prudence and Temperance, and by two scenes depicting the establishment of Canon Law and Civil Law. Poetry was illustrated in the "Parnassus", Philosophy in the "School of Athens", and Theology in the "Disputation of the Holy Sacrament".

The second Stanza, the "Stanza d'Eliodoro", celebrated Pope Julius II, not by direct reference to events in the Pope's career but by portrayal of particular historical events which confirmed the Church's divine protection. The four frescoes in the Stanza are the "Mass of Bolsena", the "Liberation of St. Peter", the "Expulsion of Heliodorus from the Temple", and "Pope Leo the

Head of the Madonna - London, British Museum

intensely human, with attention to such elements as skin, color and style of clothing, landscape and variations of light and color according to the time of day and the season.

Raffaello expressed all this through a perfect use of color and design. Strong modeling isolates the figures, whether they are shown in abstract immobility or in animated movement. A range of color that varies from soft blending to sharp brightness gives the figures individuality and a feeling of immediacy. Every figure in Raffaello's paintings has a countenance expressive of the action he is performing; at the same time, each countenance is archetypal, ideal.

The painter *par excellence* of the historic genre, Raffaello revived this style of painting and made it completely his own, and by his example he influenced the entire Western tradition. The loftiness of his concepts and the sublimity of his effects brought Raffaello's art to classical perfection. In the "Stanza della Segnatura", the subjects are allegorical in nature, replete with compositional and intellectual interest. In the "Disputa", believed to be the first fresco executed, prayer is transformed into poetry, through the waves of gestures and movements across the radiant space.

Following the "Disputa" – judging by their strict stylistic similarities to it – came the magnificent depictions of the "Cardinal Virtues" and the "Parnassus", in which, "in the beauty of the figures and in the nobility of technique it seems there blows a breath of divinity. This makes one (marvel at) ...how human ingenuity, given the limitations of simple colors, can by the excellence of design induce the subjects (to live)" (Vasari).

As for the "School of Athens", it is generally associated with the "Disputa", yet the profound formal and compositional differences between the two frescoes suggest some chronological distance between them. The "Disputa" has soft coloring and a fluid compositional rhythm, while the "School of Athens" is composed of compact groups in a slightly disunited space. It is more than likely that these differences can be traced to the impression made on Raffaello when, at the end of 1510, one section of the vault of the Sistine Chapel was unveiled, revealing Michelangelo's latest masterwork. The frescoes of the "Stanza d'Eliodoro" depict actual historical events and are executed with particular attention to color, which is used here in a highly

Great Stops the Invasion of the Huns". Although Raffaello probably did not choose these particular subjects himself, he nevertheless executed them with formal perfection and philosophical elaboration.

For Raffaello, history was not the simple illustration of facts. He understood human events as parts of an immense structure, perfect and complementary in all its parts. In his art, harmonious measurements and symmetrical distribution regulated every compositional element. Even the human figure became a metrical and architectural motif. Yet, because the historical works represented the circumstances of a particular event and individual human destinies, Raffaello always portrayed his figures as distinctive way. In their chromaticity the frescoes show certain affinities with the Venetian school, which at that time was well represented in Rome by the many northern artists who where working there. The ''Mass of Bolsena'', the ''Liberation of St. Peter'', and the majestic left side of the ''Expulsion of Heliodorus from the Temple'' are masterpieces of chromatic skill.

Both the ''Liberation'' and the ''Mass'' have highly regulated compositions. They are also similar in their orchestration of color. Notice in the ''Mass'' the fusion of reds, yellows and grays, the dark heads of the spectators in profile on the upper left, and the contrast between the light of the candles and the red cloth. In the ''Liberation'' we find another expression of this dexterity. In the words of Vasari, ''We may discern the shadows, the agitations, the reflections and the hot smokiness of the light. The light of the orches reverberates off the armor, and where this light does not strike, there strikes instead a glimmer of moonlight. Of any works that would simulate the night, this is rarest.''

During his years in Rome Raffaello also continued to cultivate his exceptional portrait painting. He executed a marvelous series of portraits, of which the most celebrated is that of ''Baldassare Castglione''. It is an excellent example of the novelty and perfection that Raffaello was able to give to the form. Here again he exercises his sublime ability to characterize with detail and to suggest eternal values in the transitory. The execution of this portrait took place during Raffaello's most exquisitely creative period, while he was at work on the ''Mass of Bolsena''. During this same period he also executed the most famous of his many privately commissioned paintings, the tondo of the ''Madonna of the Chair''.

In the last six years of his life Raffaello's artistic aspiration continued in force. Though he experienced crises, each time he regained his mastery with brilliant results. One crisis came about as the decoration of the ''stanza d'Eliodoro'' was nearing completion. It became evident that the clarity and compositional unity of the encounter of Leo the Great and Attila had been spoiled by the insertion of too many figures and by their turgid and obtrusive modeling. According to Vasari, these changes coincided with the renewed influence of Michelangelo, but it is possible that they were due to the willfulness of Raffaello's executant, the talented but eccentric Giulio Romano. Within a few months, however, Raffaello had overcome these difficulties and returned to an even purer classicism than previously. In 1515-16 he prepared the cartoons for ten tapestries to be hung in the Sistine Chapel, and painted, with some assistance from his students, the ''St. Cecilia'' (the close similarities of this painting to the Vatican tapestries suggest the date 1516 rather than the accepted date of 1514).

The ''Loggia of Psyche'' in the Villa Farnesina belongs to this same poetic stage in Raffaello's art. Both this work and the ''St. Cecilia'' are extremely simple in their composition. In the ''St. Cecilia'' only a few figures move upon a plane that is abstract, frozen in time. Their gestures are simple and solemn, their positionings elementary. Their ecstatic, rapt expressions make their emotions universally eloquent.

But this moment of extreme simplicity was to be of short duration. The works that Raffaello undertook between 1516 and 1520, of which only the most important are mentioned here, all reveal a disquited classicism, a sense of turbulence held in check only by great effort at control. The first of these works, the ''Sistine Madonna'', is a forceful image, whose power emanates from the vast movement of the main compositional lines, and from the fluidity of the color. But a perfect system of alternations governs the distribution of the elements and thus maintains a classical equilibrium.

The magnificent portrait of Leo X is large, majestic, perfect in its composition and in the harmony of the reds, yet it seems somehow veiled by a premonition of death. This is felt in the profound lassitude of those pale and engrossed faces, in the isolation and stillness of the figures, in the way the viewer's eye is drawn to impersonal details, such as the little bell.

The ''Transfiguration'' is certainly one of the artist's last efforts; the lower part of the painting was executed by Giulio Romano, but the upper part is in Raffaello's hand. In this painting Raffaello attempted to create dramatic action similar to a Greek tragedy, governed by the same unbending laws of equilibrium. He split the compositional unity in two. Below, amid the chaos and convulsive gesticulations in the darkness, he depicts the healing of the boy possessed by the devil; above, the celestial vision moves inexorably out of reach, wrapped in a haze of incorporeal light.

Index of the illustrations

I - Resurrection - Sao Paulo, Fine Arts Museum
- *This painting is from Raphael's earliest phase,
when he drew upon the lessons of Perugino and
Pinturicchio. Executed c. 1501-1502, it bears
stylistic similarities to the lost "S. Nicola di
Tolentino" altarpiece.*

II - Study of Several Warriors - Oxford, Ashmolean Museum - *Here is an example of the
silverpoint technique so often used by artists of
Raphael's time. The figures in the drawing
suggest that Pinturicchio was a possible
collaborator on the work.*

III - The Adoration of the Magi - Rome,
Pinacoteca Vaticana - *This piece is from the
predella of the "Coronation of the Virgin",
painted between 1503 and 1504 for the Church
of S. Francesco in Perugia. Although the work
as a whole shows the strong influence of
Perugino, the predella foreshadows Raphael's
later Florentine works in the smooth flow of its
rhythms.*

IV - Study for St. George and the Dragon -
Florence, Uffizi, Gabinetto Disegni e Stampe -
*Here, in the only known study for the painting
"St. George and the Dragon" (now in the
Louvre), Raphael's main concern seems to be
with developing the figures and movements of
the animals.*

V - St. George and the Dragon - Paris, Musée
National du Louvre - *A small painting and one
of Raphael's masterpieces, this was executed at
the beginning of the artist's sojourn in Florence.
Strongly reminiscent of Leonardo's drawings of
knights and their horses, its power derives from
a complex interplay of contrapposti (antithesis).*

VI - Study for a Group of Four Warriors - Oxford, Ashmolean Museum - *The influence of
Donatello is visible in this drawing, most
markedly in the central figure, which suggests
Donatello's sculpture of St. George, today in
the Bargello Museum in Florence.*

VII - The Vision of the Knight - London,
National Gallery - *From Raphael's series of
small paintings, dated 1504-1505. The composition and facial features evoke Perugino's
works; the influence of Leonardo is seen in the
soft blending of colors.*

VIII - The Marriage of the Virgin - Milan,
Pinacoteca di Brera - *The structure of the
scene—on three parallel planes, with the prin-
cipal figures aligned in the foreground—is
borrowed from Perugino. But in this painting
Raphael has used the architectural elements as
a strong centralizing force, not simply a
background.*

IX - The Marriage of the Virgin (detail) - Milan, Pinacoteca di Brera - *This famous work, signed and dated 1504, is the masterpiece of Raphael's Perugino phase. The composition achieves a gentle, sweet simplicity, while the luminous colours confer a sense of exaltation, of purely classical taste.*

X - The Deposition (detail) - Rome, Galleria Borghese - *In his first attempt at depicting an historical scene, Raphael chose a cold, sharp hue for its crystalline effect, while preserving the softness of the faces and bodies.*

XI - Study for the Head of a Boy - Oxford, Ashmolean Museum - *Some scholars think this drawing is a self-portrait, but others see it simply as a study from life. It was probably executed during Raphael's early Florentine phase, since the influence of Leonardo is evident.*

XII-XIII - Ansidei Altarpiece - London, National Gallery - *This work was executed in large part before Raphael went to Florence at the end of 1504. It is extraordinary for its orchestration of symmetrical and harmonic relationships and its delicate emotional tone.*

XIV - Lady of the Unicorn - Rome, Galleria Borghese - *One of Raphael's earliest Florentine portraits, its design owes much to Leonardo's "Mona Lisa". However, the clarity of the light, which infuses even the shadows with color, recalls Raphael's early exposure to the paintings of Piero della Francesca. Rarely has the art of portrait painting attained such perfection.*

XV - Study for a Madonna with Pomegranate - Vienna, Graphische Sammlung Albertina - *Scholars have long tried to explain this drawing as a study for one of Raphael's many Madonna paintings. To date, however, non conclusive evidence exists for such an association.*

XVI - Granduca Madonna - Florence, Pitti Palace - *This is the first masterpiece Raphael produced in that period when he was increasingly under the influence of Leonardo. His own genius is such that he is able to draw exquisite rhythmical modulations out of the motionless simplicity of the design.*

XVII - Study for St. Catherine of Alexandria - Half figure - Paris, Musée National du Louvre, Cabinet des Dessins - *This drawing differs in several ways from the painting, now in the National Gallery in London, particularly in the inclination of the head, which here is slightly more accentuated.*

XVIII-XIX - St. Catherine of Alexandria - London, National Gallery - *The Saint, who is rising into the sky, is related stylistically to the Christ and mourners of "The Deposition". Michelangelo's influence is seen in the breadth of the modeling and in the use of contrapposto, which is reminiscent of his unfinished statue of St. Matthew, of 1504.*

XX - Madonna with Child and Young St. John the Baptist (detail) - Vienna, Kunsthistorisches Museum - *The "Madonna del Belvedere", as this masterpiece is also called, belongs to the middle of Raphael's Florentine period. The solemn, pyramidal composition of the figures is accentuated by the serenity of the open landscape.*

XXI - La Belle Jardinière (detail) - Paris, Musée National du Louvre - *Here we see the exacting laws whereby the artist achieved perfection: accord among even the slightest gestures, figures in absolute equilibrium, and harmonious resolution of their positioning and movement. The human form acquired its fullest dignity under the inspired hand of Raphael.*

XXII - Madonna of the Goldfinch - Florence, Uffizi Gallery - *With this work, executed shortly before he went to Rome, Raphael reached full maturity as a painter. The use of the pyramid as a compositional structure, seen here and in many of his paintings of this period, allowed the artist to carry out conceptions expressing both simplicity and grandeur.*

XXIII - Portrait of Agnolo Doni - Florence, Pitti Palace - *This portrait, along with the portraits of "Maddalena Doni" and "La Muta", is among the masterpieces of Raphael's final Florentine phase. The figure of Doni is so strong and dynamic that the simple, treeless landscape is lost in the distance.*

XXIV-XXV - Disputation of the Holy Sacrament (detail) - Rome, Vatican, Stanza della Segnatura - *In this foreground detail are grouped Doctors of the Church who contemplate the mystery of the Holy Trinity, symbolized by the white disc of the consecrated host. By this focal element they are united, in concept and composition, with the heavenly group above them.*

XXVI - Justice - Rome, Vatican, Stanza della Segnatura - *This fresco, considered the last to be executed in the Stanza della Segnatura, depicts Prudence, Temperance and Fortitude, the Virtues of Justice. The influence of Michelangelo is manifest. The ardor that is in every one of Raphael's creations is expressed here with a new and impetuous force.*

XXVII - Disputation of the Holy Sacrament - Rome, Vatican, Stanza della Segnatura - *Raphael's narrations of a scene are similar to architectural structures: the two semicircles of the saints and of the Doctors and wise men are perfectly parallel, much like the tambour of a dome, divided into gores in perfect relationship to one another.*

XXVIII - Disputation of the Holy Sacrament (detail) - Rome, Vatican, Stanza della Segnatura - *However grand the scene in its totality, each figure in it has a precise, formal function, almost like an architectural element, and each is portrayed with remarkable individuality. Indeed, many of the figures can be identified with men who were contemporaries of the artist.*

XXIX - Disputation of the Holy Sacrament (detail) - Rome, Vatican, Stanza della Segnatura - *In concentrating our attention on one segment of this immense fresco, we are struck by the artist's ability to give a surprising realism to each figure.*

XXX-XXXI - Parnassus - Rome, Vatican, Stanza della Segnatura - *In symbolizing Literature, this bold fresco takes inspiration from the sculpture of the ancient Greeks. Poetry is celebrated here. In this rarefied atmosphere live Apollo and the Muses and poets both ancient and modern, among them Homer, Sappho, Dante and Petrarca.*

XXXII - Parnassus (detail) - Rome, Vatican, Stanza della Segnatura - *In this left-hand section of the fresco, a group of poets sets out to ascend the slopes of the mount sacred to the Muses. With acute historical awarness Raphael depicts the great minds of antiquity in companionship with the giants of the Renaissance.*

XXXIII - Parnassus (detail) - Rome, Vatican, Stanza della Segnatura - *This detail shows how Raphael interpreted classical tradition. The figure of Apollo, seated at the center of the composition, is the focus of attention. Everything leads the eye to the image of the god, the expressions on the faces of the Muses, the attitudes of their bodies, the drapery of their garments.*

XXXIV - The School of Athens (detail) - Rome, Vatican, Stanza della Segnatura - *Raphael's sense of history often led him to portray great historical figures with the features of his own illustrious contemporaries. For example, the face of Plato, whose heavenward gesture denotes his philosophical principles, is believed by many scholars to be a portrait of Leonardo da Vinci.*

XXXV - The School of Athens (detail) - Rome, Vatican, Stanza della Segnatura - *Aristotele and Plato stand out against a bright background of sky. Together they constitute the fulcrum, architecturally and conceptually, of the fresco's composition. Aristotele motions to the ground, indicating the practical nature of his philosophy.*

XXXVI-XXXVII - The School of Athens - Rome, Vatican, Stanza della Segnatura - *Like the other frescoes in the Stanza della Segnatura, "The School of Athens" is sublimely conceived (elaborating on the theme of Philosophy) and realized with astonishing compositional and painterly skill. What better setting for the great thinkers than this vast and solemn architectural space.*

XXXVIII - The School of Athens (detail) - Rome, Vatican, Stanza della Segnatura - *Raphael took inspiration from many sources. These two almost superhuman figures have their counterparts in the sculpture of Greek antiquity. The scenes of this Stanza, so forcefully and fantastically conceived, have their literary antecedents in the allegories of Dante.*

XXXIX - The School of Athens (detail) - Rome, Vatican, Stanza della Segnatura - *Raphael painted Heraclitus with the face of Michelangelo. Evidently he added the figures as an afterthought, since it does not appear in the preparatory cartoon for the fresco.*

XL - The School of Athens (detail) - Rome, Vatican, Stanza della Segnatura - *This is the face of one of the figures in the group at the right of the painting. He is usually identified as a pupil of Euclid, who leans over a tablet drawing with a compass, thus symbolizing Mathematics.*

XLI - The School of Athens (detail) - Rome, Vatican, Stanza della Segnatura - *The figure of a student leaning over Euclid helps draw one's attention to the group at the right of the composition. This nucleus, perfectly balanced with the group at the left, gives equilibrium to the entire scene.*

XLII - Galatea (detail) - Rome, Villa Farnesina - *In this splendid fresco, which signals the return of mythological themes to European painting, an extraordinary vitality erupts from the well modeled forms. The range of colors is Mediterranean in tone, based on clear, warm blues, reds and grays.*

XLIII - Expulsion of Heliodorus from the Temple (detail) - Rome, Vatican, Stanza d'Eliodoro - *Raphael conceived the frescoes of the Stanza d'Eliodoro in a different spirit, as this dynamic segment demonstrates. Here the narration of classical themes gives way to symbolism, as the artist interprets the mission of Pope Julius II.*

XLIV-XLV - Expulsion of Heliodorus from the Temple - Rome, Vatican, Stanza d'Eliodoro - *Raphael executed the frescoes in this Stanza between 1512 and 1514. The subject of each is divine intervention on behalf of a threatened Church. This historic narrative provided Raphael with the content of high drama, which he realized in the dynamic movement of the figures and in the alternation of light and shadow.*

XLVI - The Mass of Bolsena (detail) - Rome, Vatican, Stanza d'Eliodoro - *The use of color in this work is markedly different from that of "The School of Athens" and "Galatea". These Venetian tones are based on "dynamic" colors such as red and yellow on a dense impasto of shadow and light.*

XLVII - The Mass of Bolsena (detail) - Rome, Vatican, Stanza d'Eliodoro - *The new color tones that Raphael adopted in this fresco were probably suggested to him by Sebastiano del Piombo, a painter of the Venetian school who was at work in Rome during this same period (about 1512).*

XLVIII - The Mass of Bolsena (detail) - Rome, Vatican, Stanza d'Eliodoro - *The altar candles, the sacred vessels, the gold of the vestments are devices Raphael uses to heighten the intensity of his colors. The dark blue of the sky in the background is another motif new to the artist.*

XLIX - The Mass of Bolsena (detail) - Rome, Vatican, Stanza d'Eliodoro - *In this section of the fresco Raphael wished to emphasize the figure of Julius II. Thus the white-gowned Pope appears in relief against the dark tones of the choir. Most scholars agree that during this phase Raphael was executing his works in their entirety.*

L - The Liberation of St. Peter (detail) - Rome, Vatican, Stanza d'Eliodoro - *In the central scene of the fresco, behind the heavy grillwork of the prison, an angel appears in a brilliant aura of light. Executed with consummate virtuosity, it is a high point in the art of Raphael and in the art of the Late Renaissance.*

LI - The Liberation of St. Peter (detail) - Rome, Vatican, Stanza d'Eliodoro - *This fresco is believed to be the last one executed by Raphael in the Stanza d'Eliodoro. The inscription of the year 1514, next to the name of Leo X, is interpreted by scholars as the date of completion of the entire decoration.*

LII - The Liberation of St. Peter (detail) - Rome, Vatican, Stanza d'Eliodoro - *As in the "Parnassus" and "The Mass of Bolsena", the space to be decorated was interrupted by a window. Ever resourceful, Raphael divided the scene into three separate moments. In the spaces in either side he painted stairways on which the events of the rescue are logically and dramatically played out.*

LIII - The Liberation of St. Peter (detail) - Rome, Vatican, Stanza d'Eliodoro - *In this episode from the right-hand side of the fresco, St. Peter is guided from prison by the angel. The glow that emanates from this celestial being illuminates the figures of the saint and the two soldiers.*

LXIV-LV - The Liberation of St. Peter (detail) - Rome, Vatican, Stanza d'Eliodoro - *The nocturnal effects in this masterpiece, an innovation for Raphael, later became a common motif in the works of northern painters, especially Rembrandt. The work is admirable for the supreme harmony of its composition.*

LVI - Sistine Madonna - Dresden, Gemäldegalerie - *This painting, executed concurrently with the last Vatican Stanza, is nonetheless quite different in its representation of the figures. The bodies have an almost angelic weightlessness, while the expressions remain profoundly human.*

LVII - Sistine Madonna - Dresden, Gemäldegalerie - *The Madonna and the saints kneeling before her are free of earth, floating in clouds. She seems surprised by the lifting of the curtain, a device that gives the scene the quality of illusion. This work represents the final evolution of the Madonna theme as painted by Raphael.*

LVIII - Portrait of a Cardinal - Madrid, Museo del Prado - *This is an ounstanding example of Raphael's Roman portraits, probably executed at the time of "The Mass of Bolsena". At the center of this harmonious composition Raphael adds a curious psychological note in the melancholy eyes that illuminate the cardinal's pallid and exhausted countenance.*

LIX - Portrait of Baldassarre Castiglione - Paris, Musée National du Louvre - *In this admirable portrait Raphael displays perfection of form together with an exquisite sensitivity to light and color, especially in the subtle harmony of the grays. The man portrayed is the author of* The Courtier, *a book which described an ideal of courtly perfection not unlike that which Raphael realized in painting.*

LX - Madonna of the Chair - Florence, Pitti Palace - *Here the artist has used color tones to establish a serene harmony, complementing the intense vitality of the figures, while a profound equilibrium of gesture creates an atmosphere of placid sweetness. It is one of the most famous works in the history of painting.*

LXI - Portrait of Leo X - Florence, Uffizi Gallery - *This great triple portrait, with its intense figures isolated in silence, belongs to the final and most complex phase of Raphael's portrait painting. The justly famous harmony of the reds in the work seems full of deep sadness, perhaps an indication of the coming crisis in the artist's life.*

LXII - Fire in the Borgo (detail) - Rome, Vatican, Stanza dell'Incendio di Borgo - *This segment portrays Aeneas carrying his father Anchises out of the burning city of Troy, accompanied by his wife Creusa and his son Ascanius. It is part of the last Vatican fresco to which Raphael actively contributed. The fresco, which was completed in 1517, is largely the work of his students.*

LXIII - The Transfiguration - Rome, Pinacoteca Vaticana - *This complex composition, whose power emanates from the violent bursting of light and shadow, is split into two episodes, of which the lower was executed by Giulio Romano, one of Raphael's pupils. This was Raphael's last major work.*

III

IV

VI

VIII

IX

X

XIII

XIV

XV

XVI

XVII

XXVIII

XXXIII

XLVI

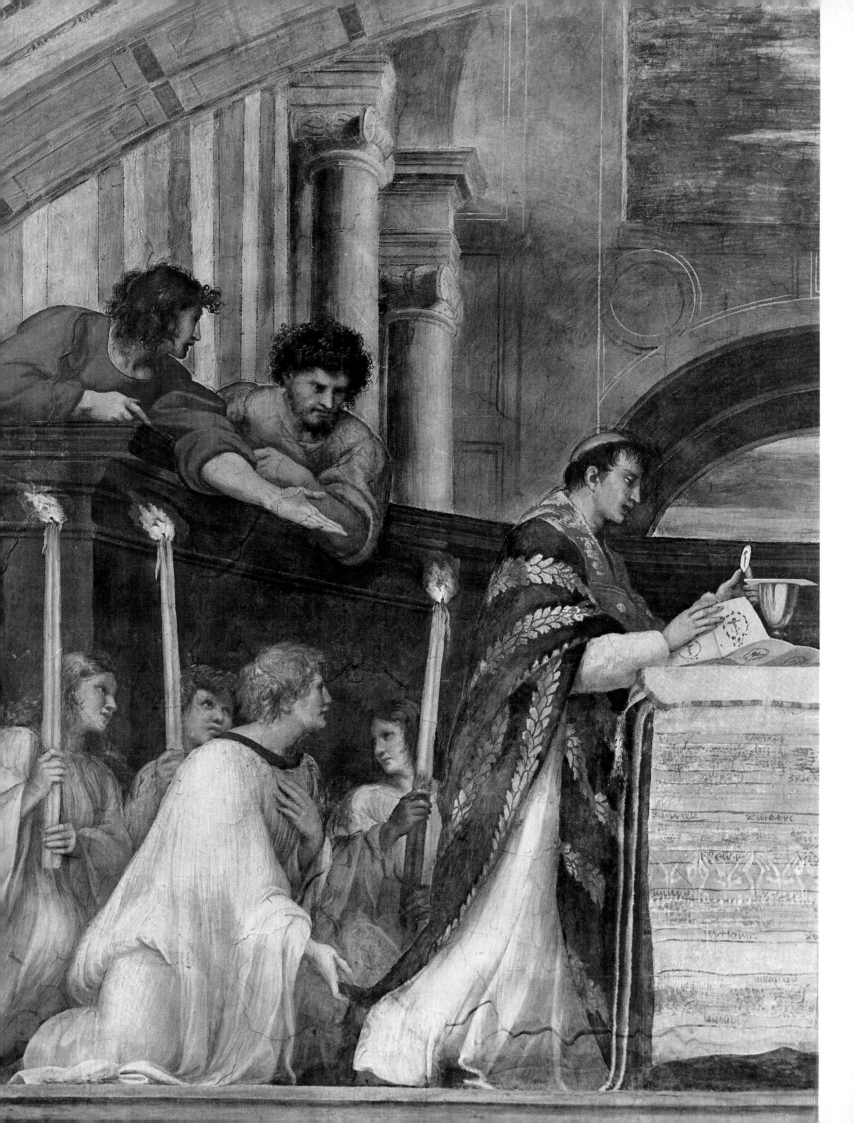

LIII

LVIII

LX

LXII

Illustrations from the Picture Archives of Fabbri Editori, Milan
Printed in April 1979, at the graphic plant of Fabbri Editori - Milan, Italy